Hellraiser's Hieroglyphics

Poems by K. W. Peery

Spartan Press
Kansas City, Missouri

Spartan Press
Kansas City, MO
spartanpresskc@gmail.com

Copyright © Kevin W. Peery, 2019
First Edition 1 3 5 7 9 10 8 6 4 2
ISBN: 978-1-950380-09-1
LCCN: 2019935720

Design, edits and layout: Jason Ryberg
Author photo: Kevin W. Peery
All rights reserved. No part of this publication may be reproduced or transmitted in any form or by any means, electronic or mechanical, including photocopying, recording or by info retrieval system, without prior written permission from the author.

Peery would like express heartfelt appreciation and acknowledge the following publications where his work has appeared: *The Main Street Rag, Chiron Review, San Pedro River Review, The Gasconade Review, Big Hammer, Blink Ink, Rusty Truck, Mad Swirl, Veterans Voices Magazine, Outlaw Poetry, Mojave River Review, The Asylum Floor, Horror Sleaze Trash, Ramingo's Porch, From Whispers to Roars, Culture Cult Magazine, The Rye Whiskey Review, Drinkers Only Magazine, Under The Bleachers, The Dope Fiend Daily* and *Apache Poetry.*

TABLE OF CONTENTS

Playin' Possum / 1
Rollin' the Bones With Bob Buhl / 3
Kitty / 4
A Voice As Sweet As His / 6
Moments Before the Storm / 8
Blue Ribbon Neon / 10
Sideswiped / 11
Tucumcari Obituaries / 13
West Side Walk-Up / 14
Inside Her / 16
Jesus Saves / 18
Blackjack & Blue Dream / 20
Copper Fox Clarice / 23
Weathered Rail / 24
Unbridled Thunder / 25
Cheat My Way Out / 27
My Brand Of Madness / 29
Seven Severed Heads / 31
Blood-Soaked Canvas / 33
Uncle Mick / 35
Paul and the Speckled Kingsnake / 37
Death House / 39
Shelby County Jail / 40
A Better Hole to Fill / 42
Death Dealer / 44
Shaman of Shit / 46
Overplayed / 48
Dosing / 50

Stop Sign / 51
Smashed / 53
Stash / 55
Booze & Benzos / 57
Dyin' Comes Easy / 60
Luminous Blue Bathroom / 63
Nine Percent Commission / 64
Even Out the Edges / 66
Redbone / 68
Jimmy's Last Dance / 70
Gospel Lounge / 73
Red Fourteen / 75
Rockland Trust / 76
Even Angels / 78
This Web / 79
Suffering Fold / 81
More Than Friends / 84
Waco Weed / 85
Six Miles South of Sunflower / 86
Faster Than Before / 88
Razor Burn Sunrise / 90
Sixteen Headshots / 92
Bettye LaVette / 93
Salt Shack / 96
Precipice / 97
Hungry for Better Blues / 98
Sonny / 99
Redneck Rocket Fuel / 100

Freight Train / 101
Squandered Spring / 103
Highball Glass / 105
Betty's Cafe / 107
North County Cab / 109
Geronimo Street / 111
Back Roads Boozin' / 113
Visitation Day / 115
Catgut Strings / 116
Lowell's Suitcase / 118
Limpin' / 121
My Bunker / 123
The Surface / 125
Butterscotch Briggs & Stratton / 128
Overpriced Oxblood Wingtips / 130
Hellfire Harold / 132
Master Chief Voorhees / 133
Firewater Sunset / 134
Feelin' Bulletproof / 136
Before the Ink Is Dry / 138
Junior / 140
Scoutmaster / 142
Beyond the Bump Gate / 144
Dead Man's Money / 146
Mound Bayou / 148
Blue Neon Buzz / 150
Sure Thing / 151
Whispers That Echo / 153
Sweet Iced Tea / 155
Becan / 157

The Poet Who Quit / 159
I'm Still Here / 162
In Trouble Again / 164
Same Damn Place / 167
Whiskeytown Sunrise / 169
Whiskey Sleep / 171
When I Almost Win / 173
Tide Pools / 175
Berwyn Blues / 176
Angie's / 178
Roached / 180
Psychedelic Visions / 183
Wynn / 186
Unvarnished Truth / 189
Ilene Smith / 192
Marie O'Day / 193
Western Skyline / 195
Song Sounds / 196
Her Lies / 198
Lone Mountain Turquoise / 201
Hitchhiker / 202
Hellbound Blistered Skulls / 204
Gulch of Guilt / 206
More Than Last / 208
Plank Number Five / 209
Amazon Jungle / 211
Faces at My Funeral / 213
Cancer Alley / 215
Passport Picture / 217
Grey Goose & Lemonade / 219

Paid in Full / 221

White Rum / 223

Glow of Last Call / 225

Scoundrels / 227

Climate-Controlled Casket / 230

Levee / 233

To Hell Before Breakfast / 235

Three Hours After / 236

Scatter Me / 239

This Poet's Hands / 241

Sufferin' Eyes / 242

Inside the Barrel / 244

Chasin' a High / 246

Fourth & Indiana / 249

Pool Party / 252

Hornet's Nest / 254

Shotgun Shack / 255

Confidence Man / 257

Claw Hammer Headache / 259

Mission to Mars / 261

Dissecting the Darkness / 263

Highway 36 / 265

Night Train / 267

Room in the Trunk / 269

Dizzy / 271

Flame / 274

Hellraiser's Hieroglyphics / 276

Spanish Moon / 278

Bleedin' on Beale / 280

Ball-Peen Ilene / 282

Most of Them I Sing / 285

In Memory of Charles Schuster
August 7, 1936 - June 16, 1991

PLAYIN' POSSUM

I
sold
the
scraps
of
my
soul...
over
seven
sin
soaked
days...
in
a
single
wide
just
South
of
Eldorado...

I'd
been
chasin'
an

old
scream
queen...
through
my
sawbuck
dreams...
just
playin'
possum
'til
she
left
me
for
dead

ROLLIN' THE BONES WITH BOB BUHL

We
used
to
get
loaded
at
The
Landing
Strip
Lounge
in
Romulus...
Then
cruise
up
to
The
Soaring
Eagle
Casino
near
Saginaw...
just
to
roll
the
bones
with
Bob
Buhl

KITTY

She
claimed
her name
was Kitty...
and that
she'd
moved here
from
Iowa City...
after
a judge
had
sentenced
her
old man...
to
fifteen years
in the
Fort Madison
Pen...

And
I could
still see
the
Silvadene

slathered
cigarette
burns
on her
forearms...
that he'd
left
as a
parting
gift...
in the
early
mornin'
hours
of
Independence
Day

A VOICE AS SWEET AS HIS
(For Freddie)

We
were
stoned
n'
slow
trollin'
through
Sugar
Tree
Cemetery...
on
the
same
night
Freddie
Mercury
died...

And
I
suddenly
realized...
even
the
Angels

couldn't
hang
with
a
voice
as
sweet
as
his

MOMENTS BEFORE THE STORM

Beneath
moonlit
shattered
branches...
we
made
our
way
past
unmarked
graves
and
buried
the
only
remaining
evidence
linking
us
to
the
crime...

And
over
time...

we
would
almost
forget...
how
calm
the
oak
leaves
were...
just
moments
before
the
storm
rolled
in

BLUE RIBBON NEON

I've been
sittin' here...
inside
the warm
buzz
of this
Blue Ribbon
neon...
Slow sippin'
a smooth
concoction
of cold
clear booze
n'
spiral cut
cucumber...
Thinkin' about
things
that are
out of
my control...
knowin'
they were
never really
mine
to begin
with

SIDESWIPED

The night
we treed
Pat's parents
'64 Ford
Falcon...
we were
higher
than the
Little
Red Rooster...
Willie Dixon
wrote about
back in
'61...
And just
for fun...
a few
years back...
we tried
to launch
my '73
Cadillac
off the
Buck O'Neil
Bridge...

but got
sideswiped
by a
sewage
truck...
on his
way
to do
the
same

TUCUMCARI OBITUARIES

We were
five miles
West of
Santa Rosa
when O'Connell
spotted
a sign
that said
Everyone's
Federal
Credit
Union...

And I
knew
as soon
as he
tossed
the map
my direction...
That if we
could
make it
to Tucumcari...
it would
sound a
whole lot
better
in our
obituaries

WEST SIDE WALK-UP

In
her
Upper
West
Side
walk-
up...
we
would
slow
dance
in
our
sock
feet...
across
the
bone
white
kitchen
floor...

Trying
hard
to

convince
ourselves...
that
good
love
lasts
forever
and
only
the
loneliest
suckers
feed
the
blues

INSIDE HER

She
would
shave
her
long
sexy
legs...
with
a
hot
pink
Schick...
while
singin'
blues
songs
to
me
in
the
shower...
And
Baby
What's
On

Your
Mind...
never
sounded
so
fine...
than
the
times
she
covered
Jimmy
Reed
with
me
inside
her

JESUS SAVES

We
were
bodysurfin'
on
Black's
Beach
the
same
sun
soaked
afternoon
a
cluster
of
skytypers
died...

I
guess
they
got
tangled
up
while
tryin'
to

shape
all
those
crooked
ass
letters
in
the
slogan
JESUS
SAVES

BLACKJACK & BLUE DREAM

There's
a
blackjack
dealer
with
blood
on
his
hands...
standin'
inside
the
suicide
lane
out
in
front
of
Walgreens...

He's
holdin'
a
Mega
Millions
ticket
between
his

Crest
whitened
teeth...
while
anxiously
awaiting
another
Alprazolam
refill...

And
there's
this
middle
aged
man
with
a
spray
on
tan...
stoned
on
Blue
Dream
in
the
driver's
seat
of

his
dad's
'82
DeLorean...

Thoroughly
convinced
time
travel
is
doable
and
that
day
old
Dunkin
Donuts
are
a
little
less
stale
when
he's
already
baked

COPPER FOX CLARICE

There's
a bartender
with amethyst
roots...
slingin' suds
tonight
at the
Copper Fox...
N' she kinda
looks like
Clarice
Starling...
in The
Silence
of the
Lambs...

If
Jodie
Foster
ever started
givin'
a damn...
or had
a scarred
cleft
lip
to
contend
with

WEATHERED RAIL

There's
an old
blues man
playin'
eight ball
in the
back room
at Felix
Street Pub...
And
I've not
seen him
miss a
single shot
since the
break...
Or
even stop
to take
a sip
of that
small batch
bourbon
ridin'
on the
weathered
rail

UNBRIDLED THUNDER

I've
been
runnin'
bald
tires
on
wet
pavement
for
forty
five
fuckin'
years...
Knowin'
nothin'
can
really
save
me...
besides
the
strength
of
steel
in

this
hammer...
And
an
unbridled
thunder
of
more
than
four
hundred
horses

CHEAT MY WAY OUT

I really
lost my
shit
when the
prescription
pills
stopped
workin'
as well
as they
had been...

So I
doubled
my dose
and
tried chasin'
old ghosts
with the
booze
again...

First beer...
then bourbon...
and when
the bourbon
didn't burn
clean anymore...
I switched
over to

vodka...
then graduated
to gin...

It was
a vicious
ass cycle...
where
the pills
n'
booze

had beaten
me down
to a
breakin'
point...
And
only then...
did I
begin
to realize...
when
my belly
hit bottom....
that
I could
no longer
cheat
my
way
out

MY BRAND OF MADNESS

I
spend
an outrageous
amount of
time and
energy
overthinking
the possibilities...
Stoned inside
this self-imposed
life sentence...
like a
serial killer
in San
Quentin...
or
Dillinger
just days
before
his alleyway
execution...
There's
a high
shine
on my

shoes...
and
an addiction
to deeper
blues...
than most
would
ever dare
to comprehend...

And
as I
near
the end...
I know
most
of these
obsessions
n'
linear
regressions
will fail
to explain
exactly
why
my brand
of madness
matters

SEVEN SEVERED HEADS

When
the
Dade
County
Deputy
Sheriff
lifted
the
lid
on
that
big
blue
herbicide
barrel
they
pulled
from
Cedar
Creek...

He
did
not
expect

to
see
seven
severed
heads...
and
a
note
that
read
The Green River Killer...
ain't got shit on me

BLOOD-SOAKED CANVAS

On
the nights
I fall
to pieces...
n'
fight thirsty
with more
wine...
There's
nothin'
to hold
me steady...
at the
end
of this
firing
line...
When
I drink
more
than
I need
to...
and my
want to
is on

the ropes...
Down
on the
blood
soaked
canvas...
with
a fifth
and
a pack
of
smokes

UNCLE MICK

My
Uncle
Mick
used
to
mix
a
pack
of
Goody's
in
his
first
Bloody
Mary
every
mornin'...
And
he'd
just
keep
stirrin'
in
more
Smirnoff...

to
take
the
edge
off...
until
the
second
Showcase
Showdown
was
finished
on
The
Price
is
Right

PAUL AND THE SPECKLED KINGSNAKE

I
was
listenin'
to
Paul
Harvey
riff
about
petrichor
and
petunias...
while
watchin'
the
speckled
kingsnake
make
a
meal
out
of
that
copperhead...
When
the
big

bloated
bastard...
slowly
slithered
away...
before
Paul
could
even
say...
Good Day

DEATH HOUSE

In
the
razor
wire
reflection
of
a
raven's
eye...

You
can
see
young
men...
just
waitin'
to
die...

In
that
Hell
hot
death
house
down
in
Huntsville

SHELBY COUNTY JAIL
(For Medgar)

Junior Wells
posted
my bail
at the
Shelby
County
Jail...
just three
hours after
I'd resisted
arrest
in front
of the
Lorraine
Motel...

We went
there to
celebrate
the De La
Beckwith
conviction...
and listen
to Mavis
sing

*Blood is
thicker than
time...*

And Medgar
still bleeds
through
my troubled
mind...
some
twenty-four
years
later

A BETTER HOLE TO FILL
(For Richard)

Revenge
of the
Lawn...
in a
warm
mornin'
rain...
where
Brautigan
stirs his
sufferin'

It's
instant
black coffee...
from two
let's be
friends...
and an
armored car
where
the orchard
ends...

September
California
in her
black bathin'
suit...

she's
afebrile
again...
feelin'
bulletproof...

N' as
the cypress
trees wave
out in
Laurel
Hill...
the lion
awaits
a better
hole
to
fill

DEATH DEALER

The
death dealer
just said
he's gonna
hang himself
this evenin'...

From that
crooked
silver hook
in the
handicap
stall at
Bernice's
Tavern...

N'
claims
his suicide
note...
leaves
specific
instructions
for the
paramedics...

The
first line
reads...

*Please refrain
from resuscitation...*

*The
second line
says...
Take these
blood splattered
suede boots
back to
Neiman
Marcus...
and
see if
they'll
give ya
a seven
hundred
dollar
refund...
to help
put
a dent
in my
direct
cremation*

SHAMAN OF SHIT

He's the
shaman
of shit...
pontiff
of poop
and
Kardashian
of crap...
His
irritable
bowel
syndrome
webinars
are well
attended
worldwide...
And
you can
usually
find him
lurking
somewhere
deep inside...
the large
intestine
of an
endangered
white
rhinoceros...

or just
North
of
Jillian
Michaels'
jejunum...

He's the Duke
of diarrhea...
a King of
constipation

and
real royal
flush
concerning
rare fecal
abnormalities...

So
sit back
on your
throne...
while
at work...
or at home...
and let
that
sick
son of
a bitch
entertain
you

OVERPLAYED

I've
been
to a
party…
that was
filled
past the
rafters…
with
pontificating
actors…
and pretentious
sons o'
bitches…

And
I've
made
every
excuse…
in a
three
thousand
dollar
suit…
to jet

early
n'
never
look
back....

Yeah...
I've worn
dark shades...
just
to hide
my glaze...
tryin'
to find
better reasons
to stay...
And
I've
been
here
before...
through
these old
swingin'
doors...
n' to
me
it feels
a bit
overplayed

DOSING

Dosing
can be
difficult
to determine
when the
powder
was mixed
three days
ago...

And
all I
have left...
are six
crooked lines
n' two
sunken
eyes...

Staring back
from the
sterling silver
hand mirror
my ex-girlfriend
gave me...
just seven
days before
she escaped
her cancer
ravaged
shell

STOP SIGN

This
afternoon
I
blew
through
a
stop
sign
entering
our
neighborhood...
and
was
immediately
pulled
over
by
a
city
cop...
just
tryin'
to
finish
his
shift
on
Labor
Day...

And
as
he
slowly
approached
my
driver's
side
window...
I
could
hear
him
say...
Sir...please keep
your hands where
I can see them...

With
his
right
hand
resting
comfortably
on
a
loaded
Glock
19

SMASHED

For
five
fast
years
I
tried
hard
to
convince
myself
that
pills
were
pre-
scored
for
the
ease
of
my
sublingual
satisfaction...

A
thirty
milligram
chain
reaction...

Where
sweet
orange
rounds...
were
crashin'
upside
down...

Just
smashed
there
to
snort...
every
half-
life
short…

And
no
magic
on
the
mirror
could
save
me

STASH

I
used
to
wrap
my
better
prescription
pills
in
a
brand
new
Gold
Toe
sock...

Then
secure
them
in
a
cinched
Crown
Royal
bag...

before
stashin'
that
plush
purple
pouch
in
the
spare
tire
space
of
my
'88
Sedan
DeVille

BOOZE & BENZOS

The
booze
and
benzos
never
really
made
things
better...
but
they
sure
as
hell
fueled
my
madness
and
internal
sadness
in
ways
I'd
never
dreamt
before...

It
was
like
sleepwalkin'
on
two
swollen
feet...
across
the
moonlit
glow
of
a
rosewood
floor...
Just
moments
before
I
would
press
this
cold
snubnose
against
my
silver
painted

temple
and
wait
patiently
while
all
the
nerve
bled
out

DYIN' COMES EASY

There's blood
On my blade
N' holes
Through the door
And this
Red lamp shade
Knows he's
Been here before

Gotta fat
Velvet Elvis
On the
Livin' room wall
Where dyin'
Comes easy...
If you're
Lucky at all...

Yeah...dyin'
Comes easy...
If you're
Lucky at all

There's six
Spent brass
In Mom's

Mason jar
And two
Dead pilgrims
Stopped short
In the yard

My ole dog Trick's
Still waggin' his tail...
Ya know...dyin' comes easy
If the hammer fails...

Yeah...
Dyin' comes easy
When the
Hammer fails…

Well it's
A half-baked apple
And a
Moonshine grin
Been knowin'
They were comin'
Since last
Weekend

No need
To call the law
Here in
Parts Unknown

Where dyin'
Comes easy...
We just
Bury the bones...

Yeah...
Where dyin'
Comes easy...
We just
Bury the bones

LUMINOUS BLUE BATHROOM

The
bathrooms
were all
luminous
blue
at the
Nevada
Inn Motel...
Where
three hours
after last call
at Sharky's...
I would
sit on
that
beautiful
blue shitter...
starin' into
the oval
mirror
over the sink...
Sippin'
one more
Evan
Williams...
wishin' my
wake-up
call
would
wait

NINE PERCENT COMMISSION

I
spent
the Summer
of '96
sellin'
pre-arranged
funeral services
in Jasper County...
And
at 23
n' change...
it felt
a little
strange...
to be
sittin'
across the
kitchen table
eatin' stale
sandwich
cookies...
sippin'
on sweet
iced tea...
While
hard

workin'
folk...
wrote
big ole
death
checks...
so I
could
bank
the
nine
percent
commission

EVEN OUT THE EDGES

The
year
we rented
Sweet's
stretch
limousine
to take
us West
to Saint Joe
on New
Year's Eve...
We
must have
drunk
a case
of muscadine
wine...
between
the Livingston
and
Buchanan
County
lines...
Because
dancin'

to Disco Dick
and the
Mirrorballs...
required
at least
six lines
of Adderall...
Just
to even
out the
edges...
while
the Kush
kicked
in

REDBONE

All
the best
pickers
say...
ole
Redbone
Smith
used to
play...
his
six-string
Hummingbird
on the
third step
of Sammy's
Drug Store...
at 2102
St Joseph
Avenue...

Now
all summer
long...
after our
streetlights

come on…
I'll roll
downtown
past the
Purple
Crown…
just to
see
if ole
Redbone's
roosted
yet

JIMMY'S LAST DANCE

Verse I

Yeah...Jimmy
Skied slalom...
After the
war
We called him
Stump on the run...
He was damn
Hardcore...

Popped pills
For his pain...
Said the phantom's
A bitch
And the
VA pay...
Always came
With a hitch

CHORUS-
Had an
Eagle...Globe
N' Anchor

Right between
His blades
And never
Once mentioned
All the lives
He saved...
Nah...he never
Really mentioned...
Those lives
He saved

Verse II

I could
Hear the blast
Through my ole
Screen door
As our rooster
Ran scared...
And my boots
Hit the floor...

His truck
In my driveway...
With the windows
Rolled down
Slumped against

The wheel...
Cold rain
Comin' down....

REPEAT CHORUS-

Verse III

Jimmy gave
More...
Than most
Ever will...
Still wet
Behind the ears...
When they sent him
To kill

Carried shrapnel
In his neck
And faith
In his heart
Till that hurt
Finally took him
On the Eighteenth
Of March

REPEAT CHORUS (Twice)

GOSPEL LOUNGE

I
was
just
sittin'
here
alone
in
the
Gospel
Lounge
at
Knuckleheads
Saloon...
when
my
guardian
angel
appeared...

She
tried
to
resign...
citing
my

sudden
decline...
and
wouldn't
even
buy
me
a
beer

RED FOURTEEN

My
first
Friday
night
at
the
Bellagio...
I
bet
it
all
on
red
fourteen...
and
walked
away
clean...
with
almost
forty
grand

ROCKLAND TRUST

I
was
wearin'
a
walnut
Stetson
Stratoliner
and
brand
new
pinstripe
suit...
on
the
afternoon
we
hit
Rockland
Trust
in
Hyannis
Port...

It
was

an
easy
score
there
along
the
shore...
where
no
one
could
dream
we
would
do
it

EVEN ANGELS

It's the place
we stash
our sour mash
where even angels
fear to tread...

Three miles South
of sawmill curve...
bloody bones
n' ole rawhead

They say...
sometimes
among the
shadows...
you'll find faces
long since dead...

At the place
we stash
our sour mash...
where even angels
fear to tread...

So watch
your ass...
if ya
pour a glass...
where even angels
fear to tread

THIS WEB

Within
this
web...
are
the
words
I
weave...
Like
bullets
before
the
flop...
with
one
up
my
sleeve...
Just
a
boot-leggers
bluff...
when
I'm
in

too
deep...
Within
this
web...
writin'
words
I
need....
Yeah...
within
this
web...
where
you'll
find
me

SUFFERING FOLD

A
number
of
self
appointed
scholastic
experts
attempted
to
define
me
in
the
seventh
grade...

So
I
slow
played
their
charade...
in
a
parade

of
half
baked
remedial
solutions
and
subtle
suggestions
for
a
mild
learning
disability...

A
dyslexic
mid
'80s
approach...
customized
to
extinguish
any
artistic
motivation...
in
their
feeble
ass

attempt
to
homogenize
my
mind
and
mold
me
into
the
same
suffering
fold
as
everyone
else

MORE THAN FRIENDS

Her
fingers
trace
this
whiskey
glass...
like
she
knows
where
I've
been...
And
I'm
still
not
sure...
what
to
say
to
her...
that'll
make
us
more
than
friends

WACO WEED

We
ran weed
outta Waco
for about
ten months
back in
07...
Just
to pay
for the
cocktail
of prescriptions...
Juanita needed
to treat
her pancreatic
cancer...
And
while dealin' drugs
wasn't our
usual means
of survival...
This
last-gasp
gamble
was all
we could
afford
at
the
time

SIX MILES SOUTH OF SUNFLOWER

When
the Mississippi
State Patrol
stopped us
six miles
south of
Sunflower...
We were
haulin'
weapons
outta the
Big Easy...
to trade
for prescription
pills in
Chapel Hill
Tennessee...
And
when Wayne
told the
trooper
we were
on our
way to
a funeral
in Huntsville...

He
cut our
asses
loose...
without
even
runnin'
our
fake
ID's

FASTER THAN BEFORE

Gin
drunk
on
a
high
wire...
staring
at
death's
reflection
in
a
fractured
hand
mirror...

Foolish
and
fading...
fearing
that
this
round
could
be
my
last...

Hoping
the
fall
to
the
valley
floor
is
a
little
faster
than
before

RAZOR BURN SUNRISE

It
was
a
razor
burn
sunrise
last
Sunday...
The
kind
that
keeps
Ray
Ban
in
business...

And
I
know
it
may
seem
strange...

But
I'd
rather
watch
it
rain...
than
ride
to
church
with
the
windows
down

SIXTEEN HEADSHOTS

They
all claim
Chuck's aim
was as
steady as
a surgeon's
scalpel...

His
accuracy
at times
unparalleled...

Like on
Valentine's Day
of '69...
when Chuck
used his
M40
to make
sixteen
headshots
in the
afternoon
rain

BETTYE LAVETTE

I
love
listenin'
to
Bettye
LaVette
skin
a
Dylan
song...

Ya
know...
there's
more
goddamn
soul
in
one
of
her
pinkie
toes
than
ole
Bob

could
possibly
grasp...

And
she's
still
kickin'
ass
on
stage
at
72...

with
a
signature
rasp
that
bleeds
pure
blues...

Yeah...
I
love
listenin'
to
Bettye

LaVette
skin
a
Dylan
song...
and
I'll
betcha
ol'
Bob
does
too

SALT SHACK

The smell
of a
slaughterhouse
salt shack
in mid-July...
can make
a grown man
cry...

When he
sees
the size
of those
maggots...
feedin'
on bloody
beef hides...

Stacked up
like a
deck of
Doyle's room
playin' cards
just waitin'
to be
shuffled
again

PRECIPICE

Here
alone
at
the
edge
of
the
precipice...

With
a
gutful
of
guilt...
in
blind
desperation...

Knowin'
full
well...
I
should've
recognized
this
Hell
years
ago

HUNGRY FOR BETTER BLUES

We
were shootin'
turtle doves
off the
overhead
power lines
with my
brother's
Browning
A-5...
on the same
afternoon
lung cancer
killed
Clarence
Gatemouth
Brown
And
even now...
when I begin
to spin
Sometimes I Slip...
it makes
me sad
about that
September...
and hungry
for
better
blues

SONNY

Most nights
Sonny would spin
Me and McDill
by Bobby Bare...
while drinkin'
his fill
in that
old green
porch swing...

And
always said...
he would
much rather
taste happy tears
in his
cold beer...
than the ones
they talk
about in
cheatin'
songs

REDNECK ROCKET FUEL

Stan says
his shake
and bake
burns cleaner
than any
cold cook
in Clay
County...

And
in less
than
fifty
minutes...
he can
take
a handful
of
Sudafed
60s...

N'
convert
them into
the hottest
redneck
rocket fuel
anyone's
ever
seen

FREIGHT TRAIN
(For Rufus R. Jones)

We
were
gettin'
baked
backstage
with
Ben
Folds
Five
at
The
Cave
in
Chapel
Hill...
when
Four-
Eyes
Becky
broke
the
news
that
ol'

*Freight
Train*
had
given
up
the
ghost
back
in
Kansas
City

SQUANDERED SPRING

There
are
heart
scattered
shards
of
spring
days
squandered
in
search
of
the
rain...

Where
everything's
the
same
and
despite
my
strange
desire
to
breathe

deeper...
the
cumulo-
nimbi
refuse
to
cry

HIGHBALL GLASS

There's
magic
in this
highball
glass...
mixed with
bitters and
neon sin...
Moments
before
I hear
them
howl...
when those
wolves
are catchin'
wind...

So
I sip
some
smooth
n' steady...
knowin'
nothin'
can save

my skin...
Oh
there's
magic
in this
highball
glass...
and I'm
waitin'
for the
World
to end....
Yeah...
there's
magic
in this
highball
glass...
as I
wait
for the
World
to end

BETTY'S CAFE

Every
other Saturday
the three
of us
would
meet
to eat
biscuits
and gravy
at Betty's
Cafe
in St. Joe...

It was
the best damn
greasy spoon
on the
South side
and they
would
usher
us in
a little
before
five...

Well
ahead
of all
the blue hairs
and Bible
thumpers...
that would
not appreciate
the state
of our
acute
inebriation

NORTH COUNTY CAB
(For Gary)

We were
higher than
the Mayor's
Christmas tree
in December
of '93...
When
we shared
that North
County Cab
with two
strippers from
Les Girls...
And
I'll never
forget
the disgusted
look on
our driver's
face...
when Gary
snatched
his royal
blue turban...

To
wipe the
puke residue
from his
pornstar
'stache...
just seconds
away from
the back gate
at Balboa

GERONIMO STREET

There's a tattered
Flag flappin'
In the
Summer breeze...
And two
Redbone hounds
'Neath a
Pin oak tree...

Shotgun Larry
N' ole
Peg Leg
Sam...
Are swappin'
Sad stories
'Bout their time
In Nam...

Pealin'
Green apples
In a blue
Flannel shirt...
He's got
Moonshine eyes
And a
Mad dog smirk...

Three dollar
Donny
N' two-bit
Jack...
Sharin'
Somethin' strong
From a brown
Paper sack...

Yeah...there's a tattered
Flag flappin'
In the
Summer breeze...
Where all the
Gunslingers gather
Off
Geronimo Street

BACK ROADS BOOZIN'
(Rural Route Stoned)

There's
Concrete sweat
On this stained
Shop floor
And barbed wire
Rash
Down my
Passenger door...

This ole
Silverado's
Gotta mind
Of her own
Just back roads boozin'
N' rural route stoned...
Yeah...
Back roads boozin'...
Gettin' rural route
Stoned...

There's plenty
Of speed
In this
383
Gotta small block

Stroker
With
Nitrous feed...

Windows
Rolled down
With an open
Slider...
Just Listnin'
To Jinks...
And driftin'...
Higher...
Cause
This ole
Silverado's
Gotta mind
Of her own
Just back roads boozin'
N' rural route stoned...
Yeah...
Back roads boozin'...
Gettin' rural route
Stoned

VISITATION DAY

My
friend Jay...
spent seven
the hard way
in San
Quentin....
for an
aggravated
armed
robbery
he committed
back in
1983...
And
he told me...
the only thing
worse than
gettin' caught...
was havin'
to look into
his Mama's
big brown
bloodshot
eyes
on
visitation
day

CATGUT STRINGS

He
kept
catgut
strings
on
his
D-45...
And
we
could
hear
him
sing...
late
into
night...
Sippin'
Dickel
rye
whiskey...
smokin'
smooth
Salem
lights...

He
kept
catgut
strings
on
that
D-45...
Yeah...
there
were
catgut
strings
on
his
D-45

LOWELL'S SUITCASE

In Lowell's
final days...
he carried
a Concord
brown suitcase
on stage
every night...
and never
opened it...
So
when
he died
in '79...
after bingin'
on speedballs...
expensive booze
and New Jersey
Turnpike pizza...
His
widow asked
the members
of Little Feat
if they
wanted any
of his
road gear...

And
all anyone
really cared
about...
was seeing
inside
the Samsonite...
So
when
the lid
was finally
lifted...
they were
not surprised
to find
hundreds
of Bic
lighters...
that George
had swiped
from famous
people
over the
years...
Each lighter
dated...
with a
name
and

location...
like
he was
the only one
that knew...
It
was the
last time
they'd
ever
see
him
alive

LIMPIN'

I'm
limpin' down
this shoulder...
two tires
on the rim...
Wonderin'
if the
groove
can take
me back...
before
someone
turns
me in...
Just
three miles
West of
Oak Grove...
rollin' slower
than my
smoke...
Oh...
I'm limpin'
down
the shoulder...

sparks flyin'
off my
spokes...
Yeah...
I'm limpin'
down
this shoulder...
fingers
crossed
n'
blowin'
smoke

MY BUNKER

Here
In my bunker
Where the walls
Feel thick...
I sit
At this desk
With gin
On my lips...

Tryin'
To channel
Words
On the run...
Here
In my bunker
No need
For the Sun...

Here
In my bunker
Where the lines
Ooze slow...
I'll take
Another sip
With no place
To go...

Ramblin'
In cursive
Needin'
More time...
Here
In my bunker
Tethered
To rhyme...

Here
In my bunker
I know
How it ends...
Smokin'
White Rhino
Feelin' hungry
Again...

Bleedin'
Black Pilot
On a bright
Yellow page...
Here
In this bunker
I'm feelin'
My age

THE SURFACE

Neck deep
internal
dialogue
unspoken
shards
surreal...
Veins
of flames
I'll never
tame...
Because
this pain
is all
I feel...
Like
boilin'
asphalt
bubbles...
or a disc
through
rich black
dirt...
You
can see
what's
on the
surface...

and never
know how
bad it
hurts...
There's
forty-five
years
of mystery...
Trapped
in this
flannel
shirt...

And
even though
ya think
you know...
That's
really
not how
it works...
Like
boilin'
asphalt
bubbles...
or a disc
through
rich black
dirt...

You
can see
what's
on the
surface...
and
never know
how bad
it hurts
Yeah...
you can
see what's
on the
surface...
and never
know how
bad this
hurts

BUTTERSCOTCH BRIGGS & STRATTON

On
Saturday
afternoons...
we
would
watch
Grandpa
perform
brain
surgery
on
that
ole
butterscotch
Briggs
and
Stratton...

And
collect
all
of
his
empty
Busch
cans...

in
a
Silver
Moon
feed
sack...

So
Grandma
couldn't
accurately
track...
how
many
Mountains

the
Surgeon
had
skillfully
scaled
before
Suppertime

OVERPRICED OXBLOOD WINGTIPS

On
that warm
Saturday
afternoon
in June...
my brand-new
Brooks Brothers
shoes...
were as
shiny as
the ocean
blue marble tiles
in Bridget's
Malibu beach
house...
And
if we
weren't
forced
to be
there
for a
funeral
dinner
that day...

I might
remember
more...
than the
sheen
on her
floor...
or my
overpriced
oxblood
wingtips

HELLFIRE HAROLD

Hellfire Harold
just sits
in the
shade
of that black
oak tree
he planted
before
the war...

N'
seldom
speaks
more than
a few
words
at a
time...

And
since '69...
it seems
like ol'
Hellfire
knows...
he's
never
comin'
home

MASTER CHIEF VOORHEES

Master Chief
Voorhees
said...
I can
still hear
the voices
of desperate
men...
confessing
their sins...
in the
rice fields
North of
Da Nang...
And this list
I carry...
with their
names
in my
pocket...
like a
Widow's
locket...
is to
help my
broken mind
remember
them
every
day

FIREWATER SUNSET

It's a
Firewater Sunset...
South
on '65...
Three pistols
in my pockets...
Too strung out
To drive...

Uncle Willie
On the Delco...
Shorty behind
The wheel...
It's a
Firewater Sunset...
Christian County
N' Ozark Hills...

Yeah...
This Firewater Sunset...
Gettin' stoned
In these Ozark Hills

It's a
Firewater Sunset...

Sad tunes
On Memorial Day...
My coin pocket
Full of Percs...
Smellin' bad
N' needin' a shave...

Ignorin'
The damned
Delusions...
Just tryin'
To escape
My mind...
In this
Firewater Sunset...
I'm
Runnin'
Outta time

Yeah...
This
Firewater Sunset...
Across the
Christian County line

FEELIN' BULLETPROOF

Grittin'
my
teeth
in
this
pinstripe
suit...
just a
thief
turned
hustler...
Feelin'
Bulletproof...

Gotta
case
full
of
cash...
with
my
head
in
a
noose...
it's
almost
time...
Feelin'
Bulletproof

The
jury
is
strugglin'...
n'
graspin'
at
truth...
but
I'm
way
outta
reach
Feelin'
Bulletproof

There's
four
empty
chambers...
and
one
still
in
use...
as
the
hammer
hangs...
Feelin'
Bulletproof

BEFORE THE INK IS DRY

There's
a castrated critic
in Kansas City...
spendin' an
inordinate
amount
of time...
tryin' to
bastardize
my work....
And
since I'm
not a
made member...
of his
circle jerk
pseudo-intellectual
band of
better than
you's...
He thinks
I'll just
sit on
my hands...
while
he spews

ignorant
horseshit
to his
brainwashed
disciples...
N'
that just
proves
how damn
dumb
he really
is...
because
in less
than
sixteen
syllables...
I'll
disembowel
him on
Superior Street
and be
back home
before
the
ink
is
dry

JUNIOR

The
first time
I saw
ole Junior
play...
was
in a
hill country
honkytonk
just South
of Holly
Springs...

Where
eight
lightnin'
fast fingers...
made six
strings sizzle
on that
beat up
Gretsch
guitar...

It was
hypnotic
thumb
thumpin'...
n' mid
tempo
jumpin'...

Unlike
any of
the best
blues songs
I'd ever
heard
before...

Cut clean
to the bone
with a
Kimbrough
tone...
It was
as sharp
as a
Gatlin' gun
through
a gravel
pile

SCOUTMASTER
(For Rob Leonard)

Our
scoutmaster
was a
former
Navy Seal...
who'd served
three tours
in Vietnam...
and still
couldn't
sleep under
his covers
at night...
He'd
take us
campin'
at Swan
Lake...
n' flashlight
froggin'
in those
chest-deep
bar ditches
just West
of Fountain
Grove...

And I'm
sure he
knows...
how important
his role
was...
because
we all
turned out
to be
much better
men
thanks
to him

BEYOND THE BUMP GATE

A
quarter
mile
beyond
the
bump
gate...
I
could
see
blood
spattered
fescue...
through
the
spiderwebbed
windshield
of
my
Seventy
Seven
stepside...

And
suddenly
felt

sick
inside...
when
I
realized...
there
was
nothin'
I
could
do
to
save
him

DEAD MAN'S MONEY
(DYIN' MAN'S SIN)

Verse I

It's grand deception
N' little white lies...
Washed in tears
And hypnotized
Telecaster scars
And pedal steel twang...
A blue winged angel
With Emmylou range

CHORUS -
It's bar room bourbon
N' honkytonk wine...
Spendin' dead man's money
On a damn good time...
To Hell...in a hurry
Comin' back again...
This dead man's money...
N' dyin' man's sin
Yeah...dead man's money...
And a dyin' man's sin

Verse II

Pearl snap denim
And gator belly boots...
Buffalo Trace
Feelin' bulletproof
A raven-haired widow
With hurt in her eyes...
Still searchin' for somethin'
In the fire tonight

REPEAT CHORUS (Twice)

MOUND BAYOU

The lanky
State Trooper
just stood
there
on the
driver's side
of my
'88 Sedan
DeVille

Shinin' his
8 cell
Mag-Lite
into my
Percocet
primed
pinpoint
pupils

He
wanted
to know
why our
country
asses
were

trollin'
around
Mound Bayou
at a quarter
past two
in the
mornin'

He said —

This'll be
your only
goddamn
warnin' —

Because
you Yankee
sons-a-bitches
sure as hell
ain't welcome
here in
Mississippi'

BLUE NEON BUZZ

It's
a
tactile
tension
I
feel...
from
the
moment
I realize
last
call
is
comin'...

When
the
blue
neon
buzz...
reminds
me of
us...

As
Empty
Glass
bleeds
from the
jukebox

SURE THING

We were
drinkin'
bathtub
beer
n' eatin'
Crazy
Bears
pizza...
at a
sleep cheap
motel
near
Mukwonago
Wisconsin...
on the
same night
Tyson lost
his belt
to Buster
Douglas
in the
tenth...
And
I really
can't

recall
how we
made it
back to
base
the next
day...
because
I'd lost
two weeks'
pay...
on a
sure thing
that never
fuckin'
panned
out

WHISPERS THAT ECHO

It's
spiritial
twister...
in my
troubled
mind
Stayin'
drunk on
dreams...
that only
cost a
dime...

It's
a dusty
ol' path...
through
an open
gate
Where
barbed wire
spools...
just sit
n' wait...

It's
calloused
hands
and
persimmon
wine...
plug tobacco...
n' fishin'
line
It's
all
at once...
or nothin'
at all...
Like
whispers
that echo...
off the
cavern
walls

SWEET ICED TEA

She sips
sweet
iced tea...
in the
afternoon
rain...

Just
paintin'
her nails...
in that
green
porch
swing...

As
sweat
beads
glisten...
on the
smooth
of a
jar...

The
elm trees
dance...
out in
her front
yard...

She sips
sweet
iced tea...
while
her radio
plays...

A
song
about Memphis...
in the
good
ole days

It's
Otis...
Albert
and
Wilson
from
Stax..

As
water spots
pop...
on her
rose
Cadillac

BECAN

Becan buried
sixteen
quart-size
Ball
fruit jars
in his
backyard
off of
Derringer Drive
last night...

And
when
he handed
me the
treasure map
this mornin'...
there was
a note
scribbled
at the bottom
in Indigo
blue...

It
said—
To be
used
for bail...
bourbon...
or that
badass
Barracuda
down
the
block

THE POET WHO QUIT

He sold
his soul
on an
assembly
line...
writin'
songs by
committee
with
monotonous
rhymes...

There's
no thunder
when
it rains
in his
heart
anymore...
and
it's been
ten years
since he's
played
for the
door...

He still
has the
grit
down deep
in his
bones...
but the
words
that he
bleeds
are seldom
his own...

His heroes
are all
dyin'
while he's
off in
the ditch...
and instead
of true
art
he'd rather
be rich...

He sold
his soul
just to
feed their
sheep...

now they'll
send him
to pasture
or put
him to
sleep…

Just
a hook
in an
illusion…
more meaningless
shit…
and a
slow death
sentence…
for the
poet
who
quit

I'M STILL HERE

I just
finished
reading
Any
Rough
Times
Are
Now
Behind
You...
for the
second time
in three
months...
While watchin'
an old
fox squirrel
play in
the shade
off Sunview
Circle...
And
as I
sip small
batch bourbon
from a

styrofoam
cup...
I wonder
if she'll
make
it back
home...
in time
to see
Dave play
Knuckleheads
Saloon
in September...

Or if
I'll ever
see her
surface
in Kansas City
again...
as long
as she
knows
I'm
still
here

IN TROUBLE AGAIN

There's
never been
a more
desperate
time in
my life...
than the
afternoon
I'd planned
to do
myself
in...

Ya see...
I could
no longer
make good
on my
gamblin'
debt...
and
was too
ashamed
to ask
anyone
for help...

So
I borrowed
my cousin Bill's
.375 Magnum...
that was
already
loaded
with six
Super-X
silvertip
hollow points...

And
sat there
on the
cream
colored
couch...
in my studio
apartment
off St. Joe
Avenue…

Listenin' to
Van Morrison
sing *Fast Train*...
while starin'
at the
stainless

steel Smith
in my
right
hand...

N' just
seconds
before I
ended
it all...

The
phone
rang...
It was
my Mom...
She said—
Somethin'
inside me
said I
should
call...
Are
you
in
trouble
again

SAME DAMN PLACE

I
spent
nearly
a decade
day drinkin'
after my
first wife
split...

Just
layin' low...
in the
dim-lit
bars
on the
South side
of St.Joe...

Listenin'
to Lefty
sing all
those
honky-tonk
blues songs...
that he
wrote
for me...
some
twenty
three

years
before
I was
born...

And
I would
watch
closely

while
defeated
men...
twice
my age...
died doin'
the same shit
I was already
addicted to...

Knowin'
I wasn't
burnin'
my candle
any better
than them...
despite havin'
been
in the
same
damn
place
before

WHISKEYTOWN SUNRISE

Verse I

I saw the ghost
Of Samuel Clemens
Playin' poker
With Langston Hughes
They were half
In the bag...
Listenin' to old
Wynn Stewart tunes...

Where South Fork
Splits the aces
Black Jack Pershing
Was rollin' bones...
Standin' next to
Yardbird Parker...
Smoke screamin'
From his saxophone

CHORUS -
It was a
Whiskeytown Sunrise
Here on Mark Twain Lake
With a pocketful of speed...
And a Ziploc-O shake
Just anchored
In Baxter cove
Three miles...

Beyond big wake
In the
Whiskeytown Sunrise...
With a hundred-proof heartache
Yeah...this Whiskeytown Sunrise
Here on Mark Twain Lake

Verse II

I saw the ghost
Of Samuel Clemens
Walk on water
Late last night
His shoes were
Painted silver
To reflect
Our campfire light

Langston
Was dealin' bullets
From the bottom
Of the deck
And Yardbird bluffed
Ole Black Jack...
Six times straight
N' never checked

REPEAT CHORUS - (Twice)

WHISKEY SLEEP

It's
whiskey
sleep
in
a
mornin'
storm...
and
hungrier
flames
where
oxygen
burns...

On
the
cusp
again...
as
air
bleeds
thin...

This
whiskey
sleep

and
straight
line
wind...

Yeah
this
whiskey
sleep...
and
lightnin'
grin

WHEN I ALMOST WIN

It's
the feelin'
I get...
when
I almost
win...
that makes
me yearn
to try
it again...

Seven
come eleven...
natural
n' smooth...
just rollin'
them bones
like there's
nothin'
to lose...
It's a tall
stack
of chips
on red
fourteen...
n' splittin'
those
zeroes
to avoid
bad things...

Done
hit twice
on thirty
five black...
gonna paint
the corners
and pray
she comes
back...
Yeah...
it's the
feelin'
I get...
when
I almost
win...
that makes
me yearn
to try
it again...
red pocket
aces...
pushin'
all in....
chain
smokin'
Luckies
with an
adrenaline
grin

TIDE POOLS

Be
gentle
she
whispered...
as
the
waning
gibbous
moon
watched
over
us...
while
we
made
love
again
near
the
tide
pools
at
Point
Loma

BERWYN BLUES

This
bartop
in Berwyn
smells like
pilsner-infused puke
and partially
digested
pretzels...

The
bartender
looks like
a Backstreet
Boys
impersonator
crossed with
Samuel Adams
ball sack...

And
when I
make it
back to
Kansas City
on Friday...

I'm gonna
dream up
new reasons
why...
the South side
can sit
n' spin...
till they
see me
again...
sometime
next fuckin'
decade

ANGIE'S

Just a
few minutes
North
of Midway...
on South
Cicero Avenue...
I discovered
Angie's Bar
and Sunset Inn...

It's
a gritty
Polish-owned joint...
where a
top shot
n' draft
at seven
in the
mornin'
will only
set ya back
half of
what they
charge
at the
airport...

And
Elvis Presley
is still alive
on their
jukebox...
servin'
as a
soundtrack
for the
serious sharks...
circlin' the
well-worn
Brunswick
in back

ROACHED

There's
a cryin'
ole steel
guitar
inside my
honky-tonk
brain...
That's
doused in
Booker's bourbon
and engulfed
in thirsty
flames...

Where
my breath
ignites
all evidence
and the
sins still
remember
names...
There's
a cryin'
ole steel

guitar
inside my
honky-tonk
brain...

Yeah...
there's
a lyin'
ole steel
guitar
inside this
honky-tonk
brain

There's
roached
railcar
graffiti
along the
tracks inside
my veins...
Where
I used
to ride
that ragged
edge...
among
other
things...

Guess
it's the
pain
of livin'
longer...
than
I ever
intended
to...
Where
the roached
railcar
graffiti...
somehow
fades into
the truth...

Yeah...
this roached
railcar
graffiti
found
its way
back
to the
truth

PSYCHEDELIC VISIONS

Beyond
psychedelic
visions
in the
campfire
haze...
There's
spirits slam
dancin'
over
unmarked
graves...

It's deep
Red Dirt...
filled with
grunge-scented
waves...
Beyond
psychedelic
visions
in the
campfire
haze...
Yeah...
psychedelic
visions...
N'
campfire
haze

It's
Cross Canadian
Ragweed
at the
Wormy Dog
Saloon...
And a
Great
Divide
reunion...
that always
ends too
soon...
Where
Skinner
shoots
the Moon...
every single
time...
And
Cody covers
Hubbard...
roots rockin'
those Lama
lines

Beyond
psychedelic
visions
in the
campfire
haze...

There's
spirits slam
dancin'
over unmarked
graves...

It's deep
Red Dirt...
filled
with punk
scented
waves...
Beyond
psychedelic
visions
in the
campfire
haze...

Yeah...
psychedelic
visions...
And
campfire
haze....

It's
all
psychedelic
visions...
N'
campfire
haze

WYNN

It's
Wynn Stewart
on Saturday
night...
sippin'
Johnnie Blue
in this
campfire light...
Got
an ice
cold
Coors
n' coals
burnin' hot...
And
it's more
Wynn Stewart...
ready
or not...
Yeah...
it's straight
Wynn Stewart...
n' single
malt scotch

It's ole
Wynn Stewart
slingin' drinkin'
songs...
honkytonk
hard...
hell you know
the ones...
It's
Missouri-born
n' Bakersfield
bled...
n' ole
Wynn Stewart
in this
hellraiser's head
Yeah...
it's more
Wynn Stewart...
till we
wake the
dead

Cause
it's
Wynn Stewart
on Saturday
night...
sippin'

Johnnie Blue
in this
campfire
light...
Got an
ice cold
Coors
n' coals
burnin' hot...
N'
it's more
Wynn Stewart...
ready or
not...
Yeah...
it's straight
Wynn Stewart...
and this
single malt
scotch

UNVARNISHED TRUTH

My
unvarnished
truth...
is
a
goddamn
liar...
Belly
button
deep
in
this
man-
made
mire...
I've
been
bluffin'
on
the
bubble...
in
my
cemetery
suit...

I'm
a
hell-
bent
liar...
n'
that's
the
God's
honest
truth

The
unvarnished
truth...
is
too
strong
for
me...
That's
why
I
weave
lies...
down
this
one
way
street...

In
my
gator
belly
wingtips...
and
Marlo
leather
hat....
I'm
just
the
blood
spattered
truth...
in
a
barn
found
Cadillac

ILENE SMITH

We
were
posin'
for
a
Polaroid
in
front
of
the
Space
Mission
pinball
machine...

When
Ilene
Smith...
really
lost
her
shit...
n'
run
naked
through
our
Dairy
Queen

MARIE O'DAY

I'm dancin'
with the
Mummy
of
Marie
O'Day...
Along
Silver Sands
Beach...
on the
Great Salt
Lake...

She's
still
quick
on her
feet...
n'
a real
crypt
keeper's
babe...

Yeah...
I'm dancin'

with the
Mummy
of
Marie
O'Day....

Just
dancin'
with
the
Mummy
of
Marie
O'Day

WESTERN SKYLINE

Here
alone...
where
the
whiskey
bent
Western
skyline
looks
like
twenty
four
yellow
roses
in
a
Symphony
crystal
vase

SONG SOUNDS

I
said—
This song
sounds
how I feel
right now...
Baby
listen
n' you'll
see my pain...

There's
a hunger
in the
howl
ya hear
all night...
N' blue
flames
in these
guitar
strings

This song
sounds
how I feel
right now...

With
Uncle Willie
on the bus
gettin' stoned...
Yeah...
I smoked
all I could...
n' now
I'm up
to no good
It's strictly
Petty...

when
I'm travelin'
alone

HER LIES

Her
lies
like
the
taste
of
tequila...
Three
rocks
with
a
twist
of
lime...

Yeah...
her
lies
like
the
taste
of
tequila...
Forked
tongue

n'
deadly
bedroom
eyes...

Oh...
her
lies
like
the
taste
of
tequila...

Virginia
Slims
at
the
end
of
this
bar...

Yeah...
her
lies
like
the
taste

of
tequila...

Cause
neon
truth
leaves
one
hell
of
a
scar

LONE MOUNTAIN TURQUOISE

In
this
Lone
Mountain
turquoise
set
in
sterling
silver...
I
see
traces
of
all
the
faces
I've
bluffed
along
the
way

HITCHHIKER

I
buzzed
an
old
hillbilly
hitchhiker
at
the
Adams
Dairy
exit
this
evenin'...

He
was
wearin'
a
Trump
Victory
tank
top
with
assless
chaps...

Holdin'
a
cardboard
sign
that
said...

Handjobs
$20...
He's
already
fuckin'
us
for
free

HELLBOUND BLISTERED SKULLS

Stoned
inside
this
ragged
ole
fence
line...
Where
tainted
blood
gets
converted
back
to
bourbon
every
afternoon...
And
my
early
enemies
were
buried
shallow...
So
I

can
sit
in
the
shade...
n'
just
watch
the
sun
bake
their
hellbound
blistered
skulls

GULCH OF GUILT

My
coal
black
lungs
are
runnin'
out
of
oxygen...
faster
than
a
tire
fire
ragin'
in
an
autumn
windstorm...

And
as
I
begin
the

descent
into
this
bottomless
gulch
of
guilt
filled
gloom...

I
make
room
for
all
the
pretty
faces
I
left
for
dead
along
the
way

MORE THAN LAST

I
decided
to
spin
Ray
Price
records
all
Sunday
afternoon...

Just
tryin'
to
trick
myself
into
thinkin'...

This
comin'
Monday
might
surrender
more
than
last

PLANK NUMBER FIVE
(For Richard)

I'm
listenin'
to
Brautigan's
solid
state
radio...
Just
waitin'
for
this
goddamn
rain
to
lift
long
enough...

So
I
can
watch
the
medieval
bridges

burn
again...
from
plank
number
five

AMAZON JUNGLE

Stoned
here alone...
in the
Amazon jungle...

With
a well-worn
wish list...
written in
royal purple
Crayon...

On
the inside flap
of a
Boulevard
Tank 7
box....

While
Trump talks
trash
in tweets
from his
West Wing
throne...

And
I chop
out another
crooked line
with this
maxed out
credit card

FACES AT MY FUNERAL

I
see
the
faces
at
my
funeral...
And
none
of
them
seem
surprised...

They
just
roll
their
bloodshot
eyes...
Adjustin'
those
church
worn
neckties...

Killin'
time...
while
tryin'
to
find...
The
faded
sign...
sayin'
who
goes
next

CANCER ALLEY

Cancer Alley
sits between
Baton Rouge
and the
Big Easy...
It's an
eighty-five
mile stretch
of swamp
along the
Mississippi
river...
Where
chloroprene
emissions
are killing
poor people
faster
than all
recent
natural
disasters
combined...
And
since '99...

in St. John
the Baptist
Parish...
school age
children
are eight
hundred times
more likely
to die
with a
cancer
diagnosis
than
anywhere
else
in
America

PASSPORT PICTURE

This
passport
picture
was
taken
by
an
ex
Vegas
stripper...
turned
disgruntled
postal
employee...

And
she
said
she
was
worried
about
me...

Because
the
photo
shows
signs
of
rapid
decline...

And
in
my
smash
swollen
eyes...

she
could
see
death
was
already
ringin'
the
doorbell

GREY GOOSE & LEMONADE

I
like
Grey
Goose
in
my
lemonade
on
a
Sun-
baked
afternoon...
It
reminds
me
of
drinkin'
with
my
Dad...
in
those
few
years
before
he
retired...

When
I
was
still
a
young
gun
for
hire
and
he
had
already
cashed
in

PAID IN FULL

In March
of 1980...
the Cerro Gordo
County Sheriff
discovered
a plain
manila
envelope
marked
April 7, 1959...

It held
one gold
pocket watch...
a Zippo lighter
and two pair
of loaded dice...
previously
owned
by the
Big Bopper...

But
the real
show

stopper
was a
mangled
pair of
horn-rimmed
glasses
with both
lenses
missing...

And a
roadworn
billfold
that held

a hand
written
receipt
that said...
'54 Fender
Stratocaster
$249.50...

PAID
IN
FULL

WHITE RUM

I was sippin'
White rum
On a
Coltrane night
Jammin'
Bettye LaVette
In the
Pale moonlight

Had a
Skywalker spliff
With four
On the floor
Just sippin'
White rum
In a
Thirty-Two Ford...

Yeah...
Sippin'
White rum
In my
Thirty-Two Ford

I was sippin'
White rum

While cheatin'
The odds
With the
Needle pegged
In my
Ole hot rod

Heard Cropper
Hit a lick
On a
Mad Dog song
Just sippin'
White rum
With the
Radio on...

Yeah...
Sippin'
White rum
With my
Radio on....
Been
Sippin'
White rum
With the
Radio on

GLOW OF LAST CALL

It's the
smell
of the
soil...
after
a soakin'
rain
And
this fear
I feel...
when she
wants me
to change...

It's
a handful
of pills
for no
reason
at all...
Like
the smell
of the
soil...
where the
vulnerable
fall...

It's
the taste
of smooth
booze
on a
blind man's
tongue
And
this fear
I feel...
more dead
than young

It's
too many
words
sayin' nothin'
at all
Like
the tase
of smooth
booze...
in the
glow of
last call

SCOUNDRELS

Most
scoundrels
show
us
exactly
who
they
are...
while
we
choose
to
ignore
them...

I'm
referring
to
all
those
double
chinned
war
profiteers
and

draft
dodging
deal
makers...

The
emboldened
extremist
elite...
with
an
inherited
ability
to
hard
sell
their
bullshit
brand...
because
we're
so
desperate....

Using
imaginary
patriotism...
cold
cooked

Christian
values...
and
any
other
fear
tactic
they
can
think
of...

While
dreaming
up
newfangled
ways
to
tax
our
ignorant
asses
accordingly

CLIMATE-CONTROLLED CASKET

When
they
sent
three
of
the
baddest
bounty
hunters
out
of
Baton
Rouge
to
hunt
for
me
in
Tunica....

I
was
already
stretched
out

flat...
in
the
climate
controlled
casket
compartment
of
that
'83
hearse...
I'd
boosted
from
Hartman
Hughes
Funeral
Home
in
Tylertown...

Just
two
sleeps
before...
they
lifted
my

lung
blood
from
a
crevice
in
the
lobby
floor
at
Pike
National

LEVEE

There's
a
stack
of
dusty
hymnals
sittin'
sideways
at
the
end
of
this
scarred
church
pew...

And
when
I
think
of
you...
it's
all
I
can
do...
to

lick
old
wounds...

While
waitin'
for
the
goddamn
levee
to
break

TO HELL BEFORE BREAKFAST

They
were
still
tryin'
to
wring
the
neck
of
my
partridge
rock
rooster...

When
I
pulled
Ed
Brown
from
my
shoulder
holster
and
sent
them
to
Hell
before
breakfast

THREE HOURS AFTER

We
were
just
sittin'
on
an
old
picnic
table
inside
the
Friendly
Tavern...
when
Don
walked
in
and
shot
at
me
twice
with
his
wife's

Saturday
Night
Special...

It
was
really
the
only
time
anyone's
ever
tried
that
hard
to
kill
me
in
public...

And
I'm
not
sayin'
it
won't
happen

again...
but
the
odds
are
goddamn
slim...

Because
I'm
not
livin'
like
I
was
back
then...
and
ole
Don's
been
dead
since
three
hours
after
he
missed
me

SCATTER ME

Place
my ashes
in a
Mason jar
then
scatter me
out at
sea...
Don't
bury
my bones
in the
family plot...
where
the worms
can feast
on me...

Just
raise a
glass...
n' kiss my
wrinkled ass
as soon
as my

spirit
leaves...
Where
old sins
meet rain...
it all
drowns
the same...
so say
the Cherokee

THIS POET'S HANDS

This poet's hands
Trace sweet warm curves
Smooth to the touch
Much deeper than words...
This poet's hands
Stay up all night
With a parlor guitar
In the coal oil light...

This poet's hands
Are on the lam
Like a redline needle
In a black Trans Am...
This poet's hands
Bleed hurt in ink
Encrypted lines
That'll make ya think...

This poet's hands
Show whiskey-thin veins
Bluer bifurcations
Over skeletal remains...
This poet's hands
Leave no lasting prints
Just chapbook scars
And heart-shaped dents

SUFFERIN' EYES

There's
a
calm
hazel
hurt
in
my
sufferin'
eyes...
that
most
folks
fail
to
realize...

It's
smoke
shattered
crow's
feet...
in
cap
toe
shoes...

Where
my
sweat
glands
glisten
and
channel
pure
blues

INSIDE THE BARREL

I'm
inside
the
barrel
of
a
heavy
swell...
Where
anxiety
chases
this
old
man's
tail...
It's
the
front
side
view...
from
a
green
room
cell...

Surfin'
inside
the
barrel...
and
outside
my
shell...
Yeah...
inside
this
barrel...
N'
outside
my
shell

CHASIN' A HIGH

I
was
chasin'
a
high...
from
the
valley
floor...
Where
the
oak
trees
are
angry...
and
the
water
churns
warm...

Down
on
my
luck...
with
little

to
spare...
Just
chasin'
a
high...
n'
unwillin'
to
share...

I
was
chasin'
a
high...
through
an
afternoon
storm...
Neck
deep
waitin'...
just
beyond
the
berm...

When
the

beast
finally
found
me...
I
was
ready
to
go...

Still
chasin'
a
high...
through
my
cranked
up
nose...
Yeah...
chasin'
a
high...
n'
past
ready
to
go

FOURTH & INDIANA

It was
the end
of a
warm
August
afternoon
in '92...
when
we found
ourselves
drinkin'
doubles
with
Karla
Montana
at The Brig
in Venice...
She casually
mentioned
a pool party
at Dennis
Hopper's
house...
and
at first

I thought
she was
just fuckin'
around...
But
when she
brought
it up
again...
my friend
Music
said
*Oh hell
yeah...
we're
in...*
So after
she paid
our tab...
with the first
American
Express
Gold card
I'd ever
seen...
The
three
of us

slid
into
the back
of a
jet black
Lincoln
Mark VII...
And
as the
driver asked...
*Where to
Ms. Montana?...*
She shucked
her red suede
Jimmy Choos
N' said...
Fourth & Indiana... FAST
We're already
ten minutes
late

POOL PARTY

We arrived
at the
pool party
with two
bottles of
Opus One
and a brick
of snowcap
that we'd
scored
three doors
down
from
the Brig
earlier
that
afternoon…
And when
Julia Roberts
greeted us
at the gate…
I couldn't wait
to see
who else
Hopper
had
invited…

Ole Dennis
was wearin'
a bright
yellow
banana
hammock
with a
pair of
gold wrap
Pradas
and sun
scorched
Panama
hat…

And as
Tom Russell sang
Rayburn Crane…
we all watched
in disbelief
as Dennis
slow danced
off the
diving board
with an
inebriated
Diane
Lane

HORNET'S NEST

I
doused
an
angry
hornet's
nest
with
a
gallon
of
gasoline...

Before
igniting
it
with
a
motel
matchbook...
just
to
hear
the
bastards
scream

SHOTGUN SHACK

There's
an
old
shotgun
shack...
near
the
railroad
tracks
in
New
Madrid...

Where
you
can
hear
Miles
Davis
play
Sketches
of
Spain...

While
waitin'
for
the
Mississippi

to
run
in
reverse
again
and
wash
away
The
Trail
of
Tears

CONFIDENCE MAN

Since
the truth
isn't truth
n' jail
ain't jail...
This
whore-filled
White House
will eventually
fail...

Keep
sippin' your
Kool-Aid
ya self-righteous
twits...
Jim Jones
was a saint
versus
this
dipshit...

The
economy...
jobs...

tariffs
and taxes...
Just
trickle-down
deception
on the same
evil axis...

So lie to
yourselves
with your
heads in
the sand...
And keep
holdin' those
ankles
for the
Confidence
Man

CLAW HAMMER HEADACHE

This
claw
hammer
headache
is
unbearable...
So
I
drink
and
drug
more
than
ever
before...

Gamblin'
inside
an
unknown
diagnosis...
Where
the
voices
are
deafenin'...

And
Dirty
Rain...
is
the
only
song
still
waitin'
to
play
on
the
jukebox

MISSION TO MARS

I'm
on a
mission
to Mars...
here among
the stars...
where
desperate
men go
to get
by...

This
full moon
fever...
crippled fingers
on levers...
white knuckles
one hell
of a
ride...

It's a
poor boy's
curse....

when nothin'
works...
like Carlin
said...
people
are
fucked...

On a
mission
to Mars...
haulin'
moonshine
jars...

in a
murdered out
panel truck...

Yeah...
I'm on
a mission
to mars...
here among
the stars...
space queen
and
shit-house
luck

DISSECTING THE DARKNESS

Dissecting
the darkness
is a
daunting
task...
As my
headspace
hemorrhages
while
wearin'
this mask...

Like a
stickman's
smirk...
shootin'
whorehouse
craps...
Just dissecting
the darkness...
in the
aftermath...

I'm
dissecting

this darkness…
in the
aftermath…

Dissecting
the darkness
inside this
flask…
As the
angel's share
escapes
it's cask…
Like a
gamblers pistol…
that'll smoke
your ass…
I'm dissecting
the darkness
in the
aftermath…

Yeah…
dissecting
this darkness
in the
aftermath

HIGHWAY 36

I'm
the
loneliest
son
of
a
bitch...
on
highway
36
at
3am...

Runnin'
the
smooth
groove
in
this
outside
lane...

I'm
just
high

beams
and
horsepower...
tryin'
to
feel
my
way
back
home

NIGHT TRAIN

I
was
sittin'
on
the
couch
in
my
livin'
room...
hangin'
out
with
the
Grateful
Dead...

When
a
stoned
voice
inside
me
said...
let's

open
another
bottle
of
Night
Train...

While
we
wait
for
the
rails
to
fail

ROOM IN THE TRUNK

This
thunder grey
Cadillac
is a
decade
deep
now...

I
paid
a pair
of Russian
brothers...
half what
it was
worth
six years
ago...
at their
buy here
pay here lot
across the
river...

They
claimed
to have
picked

it up
cheap...
at a
police
auction
in East
St. Louis...

And
despite
a few
dents...

it was
cash
well
spent...

With
plenty
of room
in the
trunk
for my
trips to
Texas

DIZZY

This
turnpike
restroom
reminds
me
of
the
night
I
caught
Dizzy
drinkin'
from
a
puke
splattered
shitter...
at
the
Flyin'
J
truck
stop
in
Tulsa...

I
said—
damn
Dizzy...
I'll
buy
ya
a
bottle
of
water
if
you're
that
parched...
He
just
smirked
at
me
said—
no
reason
to
blow
your
hard
earned

dough
on
me
kid...

I'm
sure
I'll
throw
it
all
up
again
anyway...
before
we
make
it
back
to
Thackerville

FLAME

There's
a
flame
flickerin'
deep
inside
this
blistered
midnight...
That
knows
the
man
I
really
am
when
I
think
of
you...
It's
where
truth
tortured

blame...
feeds
this
flame
And
well
water
bleeds
into
yesterday's
whiskey...
just
to
wash
my
guilt
away

HELLRAISER'S HIEROGLYPHICS

This
hellraiser's
hieroglyphics
will
still
be
here
to
decipher
a
hundred
and
fifty
years
from
now...

Etched
inside
the
hallowed
halls
of
every
honky-
tonk
n'
juke
joint....

from
Kansas
City
to
Bakersfield
and
Memphis
to
New
Orleans...

Where
hungry
rattlesnakes
whisper
softly
in
a
slow
Southern
tongue...
so
only
friends
of
the
hillbilly
howler
can
possibly
comprehend

SPANISH MOON

Inside
a
crooked
silver
spoon
at
the
Spanish
Moon...
I
saw
your
war
painted
expression
wink
at
me
in
Cleo
Moore's
mirrored
shades...

And
even
though
it's
too
late
for
my
soul
to
be
saved...
I
visited
your
grave

at
Greenlawn
today...
just
to
say
I
love
you

BLEEDIN' ON BEALE

As
soon
as my
wheels
touch down
in Memphis
again...
I'll be
huntin'
you...

Hidin'
inside
a half
spent
Diver
at Silky
O's...
with
Rendezvous
rib juice
ridin'
shotgun
under these
flatpick
fingernails...

And
where
the blues
bleed out
from B.B.'s
onto Beale...
you'll feel
the chill
of this
hammer...
moments
before
it delivers
hell
through
the
firing
pin

BALL-PEEN ILENE

The
cranked up
son of
a bitch
was
swingin'
a bloody
ball-peen
hammer
at my
nosy
neighbor
Ilene...
the night
I shot
him twice
with my
wife's
J frame
.357...

He just
stood
there
lookin'
at me
in stoned
disbelief...
bleedin' out

on the
warm
cracked
concrete...

Some say
killin' a man
like that
comes easy
for men
like me...
but I
still see
his forlorn
face...
chasin'
poor ole
Ilene
every night
in my dreams...
and there
ain't nothin'
easy
about
it

MOST OF THEM I SING

Verse I

Tonight
In Kansas City
At Knuckleheads
Saloon...
I saw a
West Coast
Bluesman
Mesmerize the room...

With a voice
Of graded gravel
Over a souped-up
Amplifier...
He looked
Just like a tintype
Hollow eyes
Made of fire...

CHORUS:

He said—
I still write words
N' some of them rhyme...
Like a honkytonk neon
That burns brighter over time
Gotta roadworn Nash...
S-63

Oh...
I still write words...
And most of them
I sing...
Yeah...
I still write words...
And most them
I sing

Verse II

Chain smokin'
Menthols
Sippin' lukewarm
Beer....
It was an
Electrified encore
Seldom seen
Round here...

Some might call
It poetry
Most just say
It's good...
Like a freight train
Bleedin' diesel
Or a cold man
Choppin' wood...

REPEAT CHORUS - (Twice)

Americana songwriter and Kansas-City-based storyteller K.W. Peery is the author of eight poetry collections: *Tales of a Receding Hairline; Purgatory; Wicked Rhythm; Ozark Howler; Gallatin Gallows; Howler Holler; Bootlegger's Bluff; Cockpit Chronicles.* He is founder and co-editor of *The Angel's Share Literary Magazine* (Shine Runner Press). His work is included in the Vincent Van Gogh Anthology *Resurrection of a Sunflower, The Cosmic Lost and Found: An Anthology of Missouri Poets* (Spartan Press), *Best of Mad Swirl Anthology 2018* and the Walsall Poetry Society Anthology, *Diverse Verse II & III*. Credited as a lyricist and producer, Peery's work appears on more than twenty studio albums over the past decade. Website: www.kwpeery.com

This project was made possible, in part, by generous support from the Osage Arts Community.

Osage Arts Community provides temporary time, space and support for the creation of new artistic works in a retreat format, serving creative people of all kinds — visual artists, composers, poets, fiction and nonfiction writers. Located on a 152-acre farm in an isolated rural mountainside setting in Central Missouri and bordered by ¾ of a mile of the Gasconade River, OAC provides residencies to those working alone, as well as welcoming collaborative teams, offering living space and workspace in a country environment to emerging and mid-career artists. For more information, visit us at www.osageac.org

www.ingramcontent.com/pod-product-compliance
Lightning Source LLC
Chambersburg PA
CBHW030107100526
44591CB00009B/309